THE LANGUAGE OF SAILING

This book explains baffling professional jargon in clear non-technical language and provides an easy-to-use A–Z index to specialised terminology.

Also in this series

Astrology
Computers
Martial Arts
Banking
Photography
Accountancy

THE LANGUAGE OF SAILING

Melissa Shuwall

Star

A STAR BOOK
published by
the Paperback Division of
W. H. ALLEN & Co. Ltd

A Star Book
Published in 1981
by the Paperback Division of
W. H. Allen & Co. Ltd
A Howard and Wyndham Company
44 Hill Street, London W1X 8LB

First published in the United States by Running Press, 1977 as
the *Running Press Glossary of Sailing Language*

Copyright © 1977 Running Press

Printed in Great Britain by
The Anchor Press Ltd, Tiptree, Essex

ISBN 0 352 30944 X

Preface

I was first introduced to sailing at the age of six, when I began to spend my summers at a small yacht club on the Chesapeake Bay. I found myself surrounded by people who spoke in a language that often seemed to be from another land. If one spends enough time living with this language, it gradually becomes absorbed. But sometimes the call for immediate familiarity with the terms of the sport just can't be put off. A spontaneous invitation to a weekend of sailing—along with the casual instruction that "you'll be responsible for trimming the sails and tailing the sheets"—is not meant to be a traumatic experience.

The terms and phrases have been selected from various sources, including the invaluable knowledge that comes only through personal dialogue with experienced sailors. Individual usage tends to vary from place to place, and there is always the possibility of confusion or contradiction among sailors in their use of specialised expressions. Such confusion can often turn an otherwise perfect sailing day into disaster. This glossary, which aims to cover both unique jargon and universally accepted terms, speaks to the needs of new and experienced sailors alike.

And don't forget the two cardinal rules when accepting an invitation to sail: wear your sneakers and never bring a suitcase.

—Melissa Shuwall

NOTE: *Italics* are used to indicate that a term in a definition is defined elsewhere in the glossary.

Aback. A sail is aback when in a position so that the wind is on the forward side of it.

Abaft. Said in reference to that part of the vessel which is located behind its widest part, towards the stern or back.

Abeam. Something at right angles to the widest part—the *beam*—of the boat is said to be abeam.

Aboard. On or in a vessel. One can be *on board* as well as aboard a vessel.

About. A boat goes about if, when changing direction, (tacking) its nose or bow crosses the wind. As a result of coming about, the wind hits the opposite side of both the boat and the sail, and the sail swings across the boat. When a skipper wants to come about, he first calls out, "Prepare to go about;" when he starts to come about, he calls, "Ready about;" when he turns the tiller or wheel, he calls, "Lee-on." Coming about is the opposite of *gibing*.

Abreast. Lined up or side by side, as in a *mooring*. When two or more boats are tied in this position, they are rafted.

A-cock-bill. When the anchor hangs *cat-head*, or from the timber from which it is hoisted and secured, it is a-cock-bill.

Adrift. Said of a water-going vessel whose movement is provided by tide and current rather than by its own source of power.

Afloat. Resting, or suspended, on the surface of the water.

Afore. Towards the forward part of a vessel.

Aft. Something or someone is aft when positioned towards the rear or stern of the vessel.

Aground. Refers to a vessel that is touching or stuck on the bottom.

Ahead. Towards or in front of the *bow* of a vessel.

Ahoy. Exclamation used to greet or gain attention of other yachtsmen or vessels.

Ahull. When the sails of a boat are furled and its helm is secured, it is ahull.

Alee. To the leeward side, away from the wind. Sails are always alee. A boat will turn into the wind if the *helm* is alee.

All hands. A ship's full crew, as in the expression "all hands on deck."

All in the wind. A term used when the sails of a vessel are shaking.

Aloft. Above the ship's deck, as in the rigging of a vessel.

All-aback. The term used when the sails are aback.

Amidships. Refers to the section of the boat which is midway between the *stern* and the *bow* of the vessel.

Anchor. A hooking device usually of heavy metal that is attached to the vessel by means of a cable, chain, or heavy line. It is cast overboard to grab bottom in order to stop a vessel's movement and make it stationary.

Anchorage. A sheltered place which is suitable for the *mooring* and anchoring of vessels.

Anchor-rode. Another term which is used for anchor-rope, chain, or cable.

Anchors aweigh. An expression indicating that the anchor's hold on the bottom has been broken and the boat is free and clear to move.

Anemometer. A device which is used for measuring the force of the wind. Some models also indicate the direction of the wind.

Aneroid barometer. A barometer is an instrument for measuring the atmospheric pressure. This particular type of barometer, which operates without the use of any kind of fluid, is the most commonly used.

Apron. The area around the shore's edge of a pier or a wharf.

Arm. (1) The section of an anchor from the *fluke* to the *crown*. (2) Also a body of water, e.g., an inlet, off from the sea.

Arming. The piece of *tallow* which is placed at the end of a *lead-line*.

Astern. Said of something or someone to the rear of the vessel's stern.

Athwart. Spanning across from one side of the vessel to the other at 90 degrees to its centreline.

Athwartships. Indicating a direction from one side of the ship to the other at 90 degrees to its centreline.

Atrip. When the anchor has been lifted just free of the ground, it is said to be atrip.

Avast. A seldom used command meaning cease or halt.

Awash. Refers to a vessel whose surface is being washed over by waves or tides but is not submerged; especially when heeling.

Aweather. Towards the weather or the *windward* side of a vessel.

Aweigh. Refers to an anchor that is clear of the bottom.

Awning. A protective cover, usually made of Dacron, used over the deck to guard against sun and inclement weather.

Aye. Expression sometimes used by yachtsmen to indicate an affirmative reply. "Yes."

Azimuth. A navigational term referring to the size of the *horizontal arc* as measured by the angle made by two objects on a horizontal plane.

Back an anchor. During excessively rough seas, this second but smaller anchor is often carried ahead of the main anchor. This eases up the strain and is safer for the steadying of the vessel.

Back splice. A means of finishing the end of a line by tucking loose strands back into the line itself. A back splice is considered sloppy by many yachtsmen.

Back water. To push on the oars in a reverse action so as to make the boat go backwards.

Backstays. Rigging designed to support the mast which runs from the masthead down and towards the rear of the vessel.

Backwind. Applies to a wind that deviates from its original course because of another vessel. This is sometimes called "dirty wind" because it has already been "used".

Bag. Sails are said to be bagging when they swell because of the slacking of the canvas, when the *leech* is tightly drawn.

Baggy wrinkle. A padding usually made from old rope and wound around the rigging to prevent chafing of sails.

Bail. To remove excess water from a boat by means of a bucket or pump.

Bailer. A receptacle for bailing, usually a bucket.

Bald-headed. Expression for a *schooner* with no topmasts.

Ballast. A heavy, weighted material used to stabilise or steady a boat, placed at the bottom of a vessel. The material is usually lead or iron.

Balloon jib. A light, large sail used instead of or in addition to the jib, for light winds. Also known as a reaching jib, and usually used in racing.

Bank. An ascending mound of ground along the edge of a body of water. A boat is double-banked when two people are seated on the same thwart, beside each other, and rowing.

Bar. A partially submerged mound (i.e., sand) along the shore, often an obstruction to the navigation of a boat. Especially found across the entrance to a harbour or the mouth of a river.

Bare-pole. The *spar* of a boat without sails.

Barge. A large flat-bottomed, double-banked boat used most often for the transporting of cargo.

Bark. A three-masted ship with her *mizzen* set like a schooner and her fore and main masts set square-rigged.

Barnacle. A shellfish that attaches itself to the bottom of a vessel, floating timber, or rocks.

Batten. A thin piece of wood or synthetic material of various length used to flatten the setting of a sail. It is inserted into a small pouch-like slot at intervals along the *leech* of a sail.

Batten down. Securing of a vessel's gear, hatches, etc., during or before rough seas.

Bay. A recess in the shore, or an inlet of a sea or lake between two capes or headlands. A bay is not as large as a gulf, but is larger than a cove.

Beach. The gently sloping shore which is washed by waves or tides, especially the parts covered by sand or pebbles.

Beacon. A signal, such as a lighthouse or a radio beacon which sends out a continuous radio signal, used to warn vessels of possible danger and to assist in navigation.

Beam. (1) The widest part of the ship. (2) A radio signal used in direction finding.

Bear away. To steer the boat away from the wind.

Bear down. In reference to a boat that approaches from upwind.

Bear off. To steer away from an obstruction.

Bearing. A direction. On a boat, surrounded by water, slight changes in direction are difficult to notice. To take a bearing means to find a fixed point on shore relative to which the boat is moving. At night and at sea this must be done by compass or the stars, or by taking a bearing from a radio beacon if radio equipment is available.

Beating. Going towards the wind, by way of a zig-zag course, or tacking.

Beaufort Scale. A scale, developed by the 19th-century hydrographer Sir Francis Beaufort, for measuring wind velocity. Stronger wind forces are assigned higher numbers on the scale, which ranges from 0 to 17:

Beaufort number	*Wind description*	*Velocity (mph)*
0	calm	less than 1
1	light air	1 to 3
2	light breeze	4 to 7
3	gentle breeze	8 to 12
4	moderate breeze	13 to 18
5	fresh breeze	19 to 24
6	strong breeze	25 to 31
7	moderate gale	32 to 38
8	fresh gale	39 to 46
9	strong gale	47 to 54
10	whole gale	55 to 63
11	storm	64 to 72
12–17	hurricane	73 to 136

(Chart adapted from Webster's *Third New International Dictionary*, G. & C. Merriam Co., Springfield, Mass., 1976.)

Becalmed. To be without wind, as a result of either the wind dropping or the movement of another vessel.

Becket. A looped piece of rope or line that is used to hold a *spar* or line.

Bee. A plank attached to the side of the *bowsprit*; through it pass the topmast stays.

Before the wind. When the winds come from behind or aft of a boat, that boat is before the wind. Before the development of triangular sails, a yacht would have to be before the wind to move.

Belay. To secure a line; to make a line fast.

Bell rope. A braided cord which is attached to a bell on a vessel.

Below. Referring to the area beneath the decks of a boat.

Bend. The type of knot, such as the *sheet bend*, used to connect two lines.

Bend on. To tie on or to fasten.

Bermuda rig. To be rigged with one mainsail, triangular in shape, and one triangular foresail.

Berth. (1) Aboard a boat, a bunk, or bed. (2) The place where a ship docks; its home port.

Between decks. Refers to the space between two decks on any vessel.

Bibbs. Timber pieces bolted to the mast for the purpose of supporting the *trestle-trees*.

Bight. When a line is doubled, the middle part of the slacking rope is the bight.

Bilge. The open area, below the cabin floor and above the keel, where water collects. The curved exterior portion of the hull below the waterline.

Bilge water. Water which is found in the bilge. It is removed with a bilge pump.

Bilge ways. Pieces of wood that are placed beneath the bilge when a boat is being launched.

Bill. The farthest end of an anchor.

Binnacle. A container which secures and protects navigational instruments, especially the compass and lamp.

Bitter or bitter end. The last link of a chain or the end of a line.

Bitts. A pair of vertical posts to which mooring lines are attached.

Blade. The part of the *oar* which is dipped into and pushes against the water.

Block. A piece of wood, plastic or metal through which the lines run to form a purchase, or tackle.

Bluff. A steep, high bank.

Boat hook. A long pole or staff with a metal hook attached; it is used to retrieve or catch lines, to fend off, or to hold on.

Boatswain. A member of the ship who is responsible for the ship's rigging, for calling the crew to duty, and for maintenance of the hull.

Bobstay. A metal wire or chain from the waterline of the bow to the *bowsprit.*

Bollard. A wood or metal post to which mooring lines are fastened.

Bolt rope. A line which is sewn around the edge of a sail for support or control.

Bolts. Tube-shaped bars of heavy metal which are used to secure various parts of a boat.

Bone in her teeth. An expression used to describe the effect made by a boat travelling at a speed great enough to make white water cut the bow.

Bonnet. A supplementary piece of canvas fastened to the jib and foresails.

Boom. A long spar which extends from the mast at the lower part of a fore and aft sail; used to manoeuvre the foot of a sail.

Boom vang. A line for holding the boom forward and downward.

Boot topping. Paint used at a boat's waterline.

Bosun's Chair. A seat used to ascend the mast by attaching the chair to a halyard.

Bottom. The bed of a body of still or running water.

Bound. The direction and/or destination of a boat, as in outward.

Bow. The forward or pointed end of a boat.

Bowse. To tighten a rope.

Bow line. A line which is led through the bow for the purpose of securing the boat to a mooring or a dock.

Bower. A working anchor carried at the bow of a boat.

Bowsprit. A large spar which extends forward from the bow of the boat.

Boxing the compass. Naming the points of a compass.

Brackish. A term used to describe a mixture of fresh and salty water; somewhat salty water.

Break ground. To haul up the anchor.

Breaker. A wave which breaks against a bank or shoal.

Breakwater. A barrier built to protect boats from open spaces of water, such as anchorages and harbour entrances.

Breast line. A line which is located usually at the side of a boat and which is used for easier mooring manoeuvres.

Breech. A pulley block's bottom.

Brig. (1) A two-masted, square-rigged vessel. (2) A navy prison or guardhouse.

Bring up. To anchor.

Broaching to. If a boat moves in one direction, but because of the current or wind, is pointing in another, it is broaching to. Usually, a vessel in this position is in danger and out of control.

Broad before the wind. Descriptive of a ship that is going downwind with sails extended.

Broad on the beam. A bearing of either 90 or 270 degrees off the wind.

Broad on the bow. A bearing of either 45 or 315 degrees off the wind.

Broad on the quarter. A bearing of either 135 or 225 degrees off the wind.

Broadside. The entire side of a boat above the waterline.

Broken back. A vessel that sags because of strain is said to have a broken back.

Brook. A stream of less length and volume than a *creek*. Generally, one of the smallest branches or ultimate ramifications of a drainage system.

Bulk. Cargo; goods transported by ship.

Bulkhead. A strong upright wall or partition inside of a boat; a structure that divides a ship's compartments.

Bulwark(s). An extension support of a ship's side above the upper deck. (The term is most commonly used in the plural form.)

Bumboat. A small boat which meets another boat at port or at a mooring for the purpose of bringing supplies or provisions, such as food or water, to the larger boat.

Buoy. A floating navigational marker which is used to guide boats on a safe and accurate course.

Burdened vessel. A vessel which must yield the right of way to another, thus taking the weight (or burden) of responsibility for keeping a safe course.

Burgee. A small flag or pennant, either pointed or swallow-tailed, that is flown from a vessel for purposes of identifying the owner, or signalling affiliation with a particular club or group.

By the head. Said of a boat whose bow is lower into the water than its stern.

By the lee. Refers to when sailing downwind when the wind blows from the side on which the boom is lying. Can be dangerous.

By the stern. Said of a boat whose stern is lower into the water than its bow.

Cabin. The compartment of a boat that serves as living quarters for either passengers or members of the crew.

Cable. The anchor rope or chain. Also a measure of distance: one tenth of a nautical mile.

Camber. The upward curve on the deck of a boat.

Canal. (1) A long, fairly straight natural or man-made channel with steep sloping sides. (2) Any navigable man-made waterway.

Canvas. The material from which sails used to be made. Now used as a general term for the sails of a boat.

Cape. A relatively extensive land area jutting seaward from a continent or large island. It prominently marks a change in, or notably interrupts the coastal trend; a prominent land feature.

Capsize. To turn over.

Capstan. A device used to haul in lines, anchors, or heavy objects.

Cardinal mark. A mark which shows safe water on the side indicated.

Cardinal points. The four principal points—N, S, E, W—of a compass.

Careen. To intentionally turn a boat on her side. This is done in order to work beneath the water line on the hull of a boat.

Carry away. To break.

Carry way. To continue to move through the water.

Carvel build. A type of boat whose planks are smooth rather than overlapping or *clinker* in build.

Cast off. To release or throw a line.

Cat. A strong tackle used in hoisting the anchor to the *cat-head* of a boat.

Catamaran. A boat with two hulls, allowing for increased speed.

Cat-head. A large timber at the bow of the boat to which the anchor is hoisted and secured.

Cat's paw. (1) A hitch used to secure a hook and line. (2) A light air on the surface of the water in a usually calm area.

Caulk. To seal cracks and other vulnerable leakage spots on board a boat with a waterproofing material. The sealing material itself.

Celestial navigation. Directing a ship's course by observing the positions of celestial bodies.

Centreboard. A large metal plate or wooden board which is lowered so as to create lateral resistance.

Chafing gear. Any device used to prevent the rubbing or wearing of rigging and/or spars.

Chain plates. Metal stips or plates situated at strong points on either side of a boat, to which the shrouds are attached.

Chamfer. To bevel.

Channel. (1) The deepest portion of a steam, bay, or strait through which the main volume or current of water flows. (2) The natural bed occupied by a stream of water.

Chart. (1) Navigational map used only at sea. (2) To map out a course at sea.

Chart datum. The level from which chart depths etc are calculated.

Check. The gradual easing out of a line.

Chine (*or* chine log). The angle between the sides and bottom on the hull of a boat.

Choppy. Descriptive of brief, unpredictable waves usually caused by the conflicting flow of tide or current with wind.

Chronometer. A device used to measure time with consistent accuracy, used as an aid for accurate navigation. A clock or watch.

Clamps. Planks used in the support of interior beams.

Claw off. To work away from shore with the sails close-hauled.

Cleats. Fittings either of wood or metal to which lines are secured.

Clew. The lower aft corner of a sail.

Clinker build. A boat made with overlapping planks, as opposed to a carvel build (smooth).

Close-hauled. A yacht is close-hauled whenever the sails are pulled in close to the boat. A close-haul is when a boat is sailing very nearly into the wind; sailing like this requires that the sail be so close-hauled that the *boom* is nearly parallel to the centreline of the boat.

Close-reefed. A term indicating that all reefs are pulled in.

Clove hitch. A knot made of two half-hitches, used to temporarily secure an object or another line.

Coachroof. Part of the deck which is raised to give more headroom below decks.

Coaming. Elevated or raised boards around areas on a boat, to prevent water from coming in or onto the decks.

Coast. The seashore and/or the land near it.

Coastal current. A current flowing almost parallel to the shore line.

Coastal plain. Any plain which has its margin on the shore of a large body of water, particularly the sea, and generally represents a strip of recently emerged sea bottom.

Cockpit. A small area usually found in the stern of the boat, where the helm is located. Sometimes on small power boats there is a small cockpit in the bow of the boat.

Code signals. Flags used as signals for communication at sea.

Coil. A line placed flatly on a surface (usually the deck of a boat) in a circular pattern.

Collier. A ship used to transport coal.

Comb. To roll or break into waves.

Comber. A long curling wave.

Companionway. The stairway on board a boat leading from one deck to another, or from below onto the deck.

Compass. A navigational device which gives readings of geographic directions, thus indicating a vessel's course. The instrument uses a magnetic needle which indicates the position of magnetic north.

Compass bowl. A container in which the compass rests.

Compass card. The card over which the needle of a compass rests, marked with the directional points of the instrument.

Composite. A craft made partly of one material and partly of another—usually a glassfibre hull with a wooden deck.

Contour lines. Lines, such as those on a nautical chart, which connect similar points of the same depth or height.

Coral reef. A reef made up of coral, fragments of coral, and other organisms. These fragments exist in combination with the limestone resulting from their consolidation.

Corrected time. In racing, a participant's elapsed time minus a time allowance. The corrected time determines the standings.

Cougnar. A three-masted, square-rigged ship.

Counter. The section of the boat in the aft from the waterline to the overhang of the stern.

Course. The direction or path on which a vessel moves and follows the lowest sail found on a square-rigged mast.

Cove. A small, sheltered recess in a shore or coast, generally inside a large embayment.

Cowl. A dome-shaped flue opening.

Coxswain. A ship's member who is in charge of all other crew members; also the crew member who is found at the helm.

Crab. To drift sideways.

Cradle. A wooden frame support that holds a boat. It is used in the building or hoisting of a boat out of the water, and/or when working on the keel of a boat.

Craft. Term used when referring to a vessel of any kind. Also used as a collective term when talking about a group of boats; thus, small craft would be referring to a group of small boats, as in the expression "small craft warnings."

Creek. (1) A stream of less volume than a river. (2) A small tidal channel through a coastal marsh.

Creeper. A device with hooks made of iron that is used to drag the bottom of a river, harbour, etc, a dredge.

Cringle. A short piece of rope looped on the edge of a sail, so lines can be run easily through it in order to fasten the sail.

Cross sea. A rough or irregular sea caused by waves and wind that are running in opposite directions.

Crossjack. A large square-sail which extends onto the lower yard of the *mizzen* mast.

Crosspiece. A timber used to connect two bitts.

Cross-spale (cross-pawl). A horizontal beam which is used as a temporary support or brace for the frame of a boat during its construction.

Crosstrees. Horizontal wooden bars which spread across the masthead in order to spread the rigging which supports the mast of a boat.

Crown. (1) The end of the anchor where arms and shank intersect. (2) A kind of knot used at the ends of lines to stop them from fraying or unravelling.

Crutch. (1) A piece of knee-timber used inside of a boat for the support of the cant timbers astern. (2) Any fixture on board a boat which has a head in the shape of a crutch. (3) A support for a boom when the topping lift is not used.

Cuckold's knot. A type of knot which is used in order to secure a line to a spar; the cuckold's neck is that section in which the two parts are crossed together.

Cuddy. A small cabin towards the bow of a vessel.

Current. The horizontal movement or flow of water.

Cutter. A type of boat which carries two headsails. A British cutter is a gaff-rigged vessel used in racing. A revenue cutter is an armed, single-masted sailboat which was used by revenue authorities in pursuit of pirates, smugglers, and the like.

Dahabeah. A boat which today is equipped with steam or

gasoline power, but was originally equipped with one or two masts and a triangular sail supported by a long yard; used to transport passengers on the Nile.

Davits. Sections of wood or metal which are used for suspending and/or hoisting smaller boats, such as a lifeboat or dinghy. A fish davit is a crane in the bow of a vessel that is used to hoist the anchor onto the bow of the boat.

Davy Jones. The spirit of the sea. Davy Jones' locker is a term used for the bottom of the ocean, in reference to those seamen who have drowned at sea.

Day sailer. A small, open boat for short day sailing. It does not have the accommodation for an overnight or extended cruise.

Dead ahead. Term used to mean directly in front with a compass bearing of zero degrees.

Dead astern. With a zero degree bearing or reading, referring to directly behind the vessel.

Dead flat. The widest part of a ship; a term used in shipbuilding.

Dead reckoning. To fix a course by compass, speed, and current readings according to the ship's log as opposed to using astronomical readings.

Dead rise. The distance between the ship's keel and the beams found amidship. A term used in shipbuilding.

Dead sheave. An opening at the heel of the mast through which an additional tackle can be run.

Deadeye. A wooden block through which the *lanyards* run in order to extend or stretch the stays, shroud, and other parts of boat's rigging.

Deadhead. A block of wood used as a buoy for an anchor; a submerged mast.

Deadlight. A strong piece of glass fixed in a deck or on the side of a ship. Also, a shutter which fits over a cabin porthole to seal the cabin against any possible water leakage during rough seas.

Deadwater. Water which whirls around the stern of a boat as it travels. Also called eddy water.

Deadwood. Blocks of wood at the keel and towards the stern.

Deck. The vessel's platform, or floor.

Deck head. The underside of the deck.

Deck beam. A timber which spans across the ship within its framework as a support for the deck.

Deck hand. A member of the crew who works on or about the decks of a ship.

Deep. (1) Generally referring to depths which are greater than 3000 *fathoms*. (2) Any mark found between two fathom points as read on a sounding line.

Degauss. To neutralise or demagnetise the magnetic field found around a ship.

Delta. The low alluvial land, deposited in a more or less triangular form, at the mouth of a river.

Departure. A ship's course or position at her starting point. It is read in latitude and longitude.

Derelict. A ship which has been abandoned at sea.

Derrick. An instrument that is used for moving and hoisting heavy weights. It is made of a stationary, vertical timber and a long moving timber which moves from the base of the stationary beam.

Deviation. A mistake in the compass readings caused by the influence of magnetic forces.

Dew point. That point at which there is enough moisture in the air to create fog.

Dinghy. A small boat often used to transport passengers or crew members from a mooring to shore. Often rigged for sailing.

Dip. To lower and then re-hoist an ensign.

Dismast. The breaking, or the carrying away of a mast; for example, a boat being dismasted by the force of a storm.

Displacement. The weight of that water which is displaced by a boat.

Ditty bag. A small bag used to hold personal belongings; it is usually made of canvas.

Dividers. A charting device used to mark off distances.

Dock. A structure used for the securing of a vessel to a landing, pier, or wharf. Dockage is that fee which one pays in order to use a dock.

Dogwatch. Duty time aboard a boat divides the day into seven periods. Two of the periods are only two hours long—from 4 to 6 pm and from 6 to 8 pm—as opposed to the four hours of the other duty periods. These shorter watches are dog-watches.

Dolphin. A *piling* found at the entrance to a dock; also, a spar made fast to an anchor.

Dolphin striker. Also called martingale, a spar which is located beneath the boat's bowsprit forming a support for the jib.

Dory. A very seaworthy rowboat with a narrow, flat bottom, high bow, and flaring sides.

Double-ender. A sailboat with a pointed bow and stern.

Douse, dowse. To suddenly slacken and lower a sail. To extinguish a light. To soak with water.

Down-haul. A rope pulling downwards.

Down-helm. To sail away from the wind.

Drag. A type of anchor which floats, and is sometimes used to keep a ship's head pointed in the wind. Also, the drag is the difference found between the draught of the fore and aft of a boat.

Draught. The draught of a boat is the distance from the waterline to the tip of the hull or keel. This measurement is equal to the smallest depth of water in which a boat can travel.

Drawn. Sails filled with wind are said to be drawn.

Dredge. See *creeper*.

Drift. The action of a boat as it moves along in its course because of the force of winds, currents, or tides.

Drift anchor. A drag anchor.

Driver. A large sail set at the stern of a boat.

Drop. A sail's depth from head to foot. Also, to release an anchor is to drop an anchor.

Drouge. A sea-anchor or buoy; it is used when travelling to create a certain amount of drag.

Dry dock. An artificial basin fitted with a gate or caisson into which a vessel may be floated and from which the water may be pumped out to expose the bottom of the vessel. It is used for repairing, building, and painting boats. Sometimes referred to as a graving dock.

Dry rot. Damage to the wood of a vessel because of a fungus growth. The term, dry, is somewhat inaccurate since moisture is necessary for the decay-causing fungus to grow.

Duck. A light material of cotton or linen used in the making of small sails.

Earing. A small rope that is attached to the sail in order to bend or *reef* it.

Ease. To decrease the pressure on a sail by letting out the *sheet*.

Easting. The distance which a boat travels, or the distance gained when travelling on an easterly course.

Ebb. The receding of the tide.

Echo-sounder. Instrument used for determining the depth of water beneath the boat.

Eddy. A small whirlpool caused by the meeting of opposing currents.

Ensign. A flag displayed in order to indicate the nationality of a ship.

Equinox. Two days of the year that have equal hours of daylight and darkness. The Spring equinox occurs near the end of March; the Autumnal equinox occurs near the end of September.

Even keel. The position a boat is in when she sits evenly in the water, with neither bow nor stern higher than the other.

Eye of the storm. The relatively calm weather in the centre of a severe tropical cyclone.

Eye of the wind. The exact direction from which the wind is blowing.

Eyes. The most forward section of the boat's deck. Also the section of a shroud which goes over the mast.

Eyesplice. A *splice* made by doubling back a line and splicing it again.

Fag end or fagged. A line is fagged when its end is frayed or unravelled.

Fair lead. A block of wood or metal through which lines and rigging run easily.

Fairway. An open and navigable body of water.

Fairwind. A wind which is travelling on the same course as the boat.

Fall. Lines used for hoisting and lowering a boat.

Fall astern. In passing another vessel and making the distance between the two boats greater, the passed boat is said to fall astern.

Fall off. To steer the boat away from the direction of the wind.

False keel. An additional extension keel used for stability and increased draught.

Fanning. The slight movement of a sailboat in light winds.

Fashion timber. That timber which is specially structured to form the stern.

Fast. To secure, as in a line, to make fast.

Fathom. A unit of measurement used to determine water depth. One fathom equals 6 feet.

Feather. To turn an oar so that its blade is parallel to the water. When the blade is in the water this action reduces water resistance. When the blade is in the air, the action reduces wind resistance and makes water run off an oar in a feather-like spray. Also, to ease up on a sail to allow wind to spill.

Fend off. To clear a dock or another vessel by pushing off from it.

Fender. Protective padding gear placed on the sides of a vessel, when docking or mooring with another vessel. Sometimes, on larger boats, these fenders are made of heavy, thick rope; on smaller boats, they are often pads stuffed with cork or other materials which float.

Fetch. To reach a destination.

Fiddle. The railing on a table on board a boat which keeps pots, pans, dishes, etc., from falling during heavy seas and high winds.

Fiddle block. A block found on the rigging; it is made of two sheaves, the upper being larger than the smaller.

Figurehead. A carved figure or bust extending over the bow of the boat. According to legend, they were used to scare away evil sea spirits.

Fish. A purchase used to hoist an anchor to the boat's edge.

Fit. To equip or prepare a boat with provisions for a long cruise.

Fix. To make a stable determination of a vessel's position via observation of the ship and/or surroundings, radio, or any other reliable means.

Flare. A vessel's upward and outward curves. Also, a burning material or light used as a signal, usually in an emergency.

Flashing. A navigational light that flashes on at intervals, the periods of light being shorter than the periods of darkness.

Flat. When a *sheet* is hauled down close, it is said to be drawn flat.

Fleet. A group of boats usually organised under one commanding officer.

Flood. The incoming tide. The opposite of ebb.

Flood anchor. During a flood tide, an anchor that is used to stabilise the boat.

Floor. The bed or bottom of the ocean.

Floor timber. In shipbuilding, the *timbers* upon which the floor is laid; one, in particular, is immediately placed across the keel of the boat.

Floorboards. Wooden slats used to protect the bottom of a boat. They lie lengthwise along the floor of a boat and may sometimes be removed.

Flotation. Materials or air tight tanks which are built into a boat to prevent it from sinking.

Flotsam. The floating remains of a ship and its cargo after a destructive storm or a shipwreck.

Flowing sheet. When sails are loose and flowing freely for the purpose of catching more wind.

Fluke. The part of the anchor that is triangular and pointed, and grabs the bottom.

Flush. A level deck design that has no mast housing above deck.

Fly. Flag's end which extends out from the *halyards*; it indicates the direction in which the wind is blowing.

Fog. At the *dew point*, a vapour which is composed of water particles. Fog differs from a cloud only in that it is located close to the ground. It is therefore a hazard to ships as it reduces and often totally obscures visibility.

Following sea. When waves approach a boat from its stern.

Foot. The bottom end of a sail or mast.

Footrope. A cable which is stretched across the *yard* for members of the crew to stand on while *furling* or *reefing* a sail.

Footwaling. The hull's inside lining which spans to the lower deck.

Fore. Refers to the front section of a boat.

Fore and aft. The whole boat. The expression refers to the front and rear sections of a vessel, respectively.

Fore sail. The main, square sail found on the *foremast* of a boat.

Forecastle (pron. *fo'c'sl*). The compartment most forward in a boat, below the deck, containing the living quarters.

Forefoot. The section of a vessel where the keel and the stem of the boat intersect.

Foremast. The mast found closest to the bow of a boat.

Forereach. To overtake another boat.

Fore-runner. A piece of material attached to the *log line* in order to measure the limit of the *drift-line*.

Forward. The area towards the bow of a boat.

Foul. To be obstructed or tangled in some way, e.g. anchor fouled.

Foul hawse. The twisted line, or cable, of an anchor.

Found. To be equipped. If a vessel is equipped exceptionally well, she is "well-founded."

Founder. To sink a vessel by filling it with water.

Fractional rig. Where forestay runs only part way up the mast, not to the masthead.

Frames. The ribs which define a boat's basic structure or skeleton.

Frap. To add strength by tying together cables or lines.

Free. Describes the movement of a boat which travels with a good wind and no obstacles.

Freeboard. The section of a boat, between the hull's waterline and the boat's deck, which remains above the water.

Fresh breeze. Wind with a velocity between 17 and 20 knots.

Fresh water. Water which contains no salt.

Freshen. When the wind picks up strength.

Full spread. Expression signifying all sails up.

Furl. To tightly roll up a sail. When sails are lowered, they must be furled and then secured to the *boom*. This protects the sails and preserves the neat appearance of a ship.

Futtock. A part of the boat's skeleton which forms one of the upward curves of the boat's *ribs*.

Futtock hoop. The band which holds the futtock shrouds in place. It is located around the mast.

Futtock plate. An iron plate which holds the *futtock shrouds*. It is placed horizontally on the lower mast of a boat.

Futtock shrouds. Short, heavy iron lines that connect the *futtock plates* with the lower mast.

Gaff. A small *spar* on which the fore and aft sails are extended; hence, the expression "gaff-rigged," (as opposed to Bermuda rig.)

Gaff-topsail. A small, light sail rigged above a *gaff*.

Gale. Wind of force 8 or 9 on the Beaufort scale.

Galley. Name given to the kitchen on a boat.

Gallow bitts. A strong frame which is erected in order to hold additional spars that are located amidships. Also termed gallows frame.

Gammon. The bands by which the *bowsprit* is lashed to the *stem* of the boat.

Gammon plate. The iron plate located on the stem of the boat, and to which gammon shackles are secured.

Gammon shackles. Chains or ropes which are used to secure the *gammon*.

Gangplank. A moveable bridge which extends from a vessel to a dock or pier. It functions as a passageway from ship to shore.

Gangway. (1) A passageway on the side of a boat through which people enter, leave, or on which they move about. (2) If shouted, it means "Get out of the way!"

Garboard strake. A section of planking located on both sides of the keel.

Garland. A loop of rope used to hoist or raise spars.

Garnet. A *tackle* which is used for hoisting. It is located on the mainstay.

Gaskets. Straps that are wrapped around sails so that they remain furled.

Gauge. The degree to which a boat is submerged in water when fully loaded.

Gayyou. An Annamese (of the Mongoloid race) fishing boat that is narrow and flat-bottomed. It has either a two or three masted rigger, and a portable cabin cover.

Gear. General term referring to all the equipment found on board a boat, including the rigging.

Genoa. A large *jib* which overlaps the *mainsail.* It is also called a "Jenny."

Ghosting. To sail when there is little or no wind. A Ghoster is a sailboat that makes comparatively good way in light wind.

Gibe. If, when a boat changes direction, its stern or back end crosses the wind, the boat gibes. It then takes the wind on the opposite side of the boat and the sails, and the sails cross the boat. Gibing is the opposite of coming about; it is easier to do, but more dangerous, because of the speed and force with which the sails cross the boat. Many small craft have been capsized and sailors lost due to inexpert gibing. A skipper's final warning before he gibes is, "Gibe ho!"

Gig. A long boat rigged with sails as well as oars. It is one of a larger ship's boats, and is usually reserved for an officer.

Gimbal. A device made of brass which stabilises and balances gear (a stove or compass, for example) should a vessel deviate from an upright position.

Girt. To moor a boat on either side by two cables whose anchors are attached. This method of mooring prevents the boat from swaying back and forth.

Girtline. A line used to hoist the rigging up to the masthead.

Give way. A command given to crew members, usually oarsmen, to increase the power of their strokes. Also, an order to stay clear of another vessel.

Glass. Refers to a barometer or a pair of binoculars.

Go about. To tack, to change direction across the wind.

Gobline. A line which leads inward from the *martingale*.

Gooseneck. Metal fitting which secures the boom to the mast.

Goose winged. Sailing with the wind aft, with the foresail on one side of the boat and the mainsail on the other.

Gore. A section of material which increases the width or length of a sail.

Grafting. To strengthen or cover a rope by twisting or weaving strands of line together.

Granny knot. A *square knot* which is tied improperly by crossing the ends in the wrong fashion. This knot is far less secure than a square knot.

Grapnel. A small anchor with four or five *flukes*. It is used for anchoring small boats.

Grappling iron. A long iron with protruding hooks. It is dragged along the floor of a body of water in order to recover lost objects.

Grating. Open metal- or woodwork which covers the *hatches* of a boat; also a removable floor, or section of a floor which may be removed.

Greave. Refers to the cleaning of the bottom of a boat. The task is often accomplished by burning.

Grommet. A loop of line which secures a sail.

Ground swell. A broad swell of the water, often caused by distant gales and other weather disturbances.

Ground tackle. An all-inclusive term referring to the gear used in the mooring and anchoring of a vessel.

Gudgeon. A *rudder* support.

Gulf. A part of an ocean or sea extending into the land, usually larger than a bay.

Gunwale (*or* gunnel). The upper edge of a boat's side.

Gust. A brief burst of wind.

Guy. A line used to stabilise anything found on board a boat.

Hail. To greet or signal other boats or boaters.

Halyards. Lines and cables used for hoisting and lowering sails and other rigging found on board. Also spelled halliards or haliards.

Hammock. Stretched and hung canvas which is often used as sleeping quarters.

Hand. A crew member.

Handsomely. Describes the movement of a vessel when it is sailed carefully and steadily.

Handspike. A lever, usually made of wood, that is used to heave heavy objects.

Hank. A band of wood or metal around the edge of the *staysail*.

Harbour. A water area nearly surrounded by land or artificial dikes, providing a safe anchorage for boats.

Hard. An area for beaching boats.

Harpoon. A spear used for stabbing large fish.

Hard a starboard/port. The use of maximum helm in the required direction.

Hatch. An opening in the deck which allows air to circulate in the cabin. It also functions as a passageway to and from the cabin.

Hatch-bar. A bar made of iron which secures the hatches when necessary.

Haul. (1) Refers to a wind which changes direction. (2) To pull in a line.

Hawse. An area between the bow and the anchor.

Hawse bolster. A piece or block of iron which protects the hawsehole from the chafing action of the line or cable that runs through it.

Hawse piece. The beams in the bow of the boat in which the hawsehole is cut.

Hawsehole. A hole in the bow of the boat which allows the free passage of an anchor line or cable.

Hawsepipe. An iron pipe that is placed inside of the hawsehole to prevent the wood of the bow of the boat from eroding.

Hawser. A long, thick rope used mostly on larger ships; sometimes used as an anchor line on smaller boats.

Haze. A punishment of unduly hard labour that is inflicted upon a sailor.

Head. (1) A nautical term referring to a toilet on board a boat. (2) Also refers to the bow, or most forward part of a boat. The expression "by the head" describes the bow of a boat when it is submerged more deeply than the stern.

Head room. The height of the area located below decks.

Head wind. A wind which is blowing in a direction that is opposite from that in which the boat is travelling.

Heading. The direction in which a boat is moving.

Headsails (pron. *heads'ls*). The sails which are located closest to the front of the boat.

Headsea. When waves are coming from ahead. The opposite of a *following sea*.

Headway. The forward movement of a boat, usually to a particular destination.

Heave. To throw or toss a line.

Heave ho! An exclamation which accompanies the hoisting of an anchor or any other heavy piece of equipment.

Heave to. To steer a boat into the wind so that it comes to a halt.

Heave short. To haul in a cable to the extent that it brings the boat over the anchor.

Heaving line. A light line with a weight on its end for throwing to someone on shore.

Heel. The position of a boat when it leans over and travels on one side. In a good wind, a boat can heel over to the extent that it forms a 45 degree angle with the water. Also refers to the rear or aft section of the keel.

Heeling error. A misreading of the compass because of a failure to account for the change in position when a boat is heeling.

Helm. The equipment used to direct or steer the boat, such as the tiller or wheel.

Helm amidships. A command meaning "keep a straight course." In steering a boat, the helmsman controls the tiller (or wheel in larger vessels) which is attached to a rudder; it is the rudder which directs the boat. Helm amidships indicates that the rudder is parallel to the centreline of the boat, and the boat is going straight. This command is usually given when a turning vessel is pointing towards its destination.

Helmsman. The person who is stationed at the helm and is in charge of steering the boat.

High and dry. The condition of a boat when she is aground and above the watermark.

Hike. See *leaning out*.

Hiking stick. See *tiller extension*.

Hiking strap. See *toe strap*.

Hitch. A knot or another way of securing equipment, supplies, or other materials in a boat.

Hold. The interior section of a boat that is located below decks.

Hold water. To position the oars such that they stop the boat. This result is accomplished by placing the blades of the oars in the water so that they are perpendicular to the water line. The oars therefore resist the flow of water and bring the boat to a halt.

Holiday. Any section of a boat that is accidentally missed in the process of varnishing and/or painting.

Holy-stone. A stone which is used to scrub the decks. The device is so named because decks were traditionally scrubbed on Sundays.

Hood. A covering which fits over the *companionway*.

Horizon. The apparent intersection of water and sky.

Horns. *Cleat* arms around which lines are coiled and knotted, thereby securing them.

Hourglass. A *spinnaker* twisted in the middle so the wind fills the bottom and top parts separately.

House. The portion of the mast located below deck.

House flag. Owner's flag.

Hull. The frame or body of a vessel. This does not include the mast, sails, decks or rigging.

Inboard. The area of a vessel that lies inside the hull, or towards the centreline. Also, a motor that is mounted on the inside of a boat.

Inlet. A narrow waterway or a gap in the land that connects a small body of water with a larger one; a small narrow bay or creek.

Inshore. A directional term which means towards the shore.

Irons. When a boat is pointed dead into the wind and can't get out of it, it is in irons. This often happens when a sailboat tries to *come about* with insufficient speed. Boats moored or at anchor naturally point directly into the wind.

Island. A body of land extending above, and completely surrounded by, water; an area of swamp entirely surrounded by open water.

Islet. A small island.

Isophase. A navigational light that flashes on and off with equal periods of light and darkness.

Isthmus. A narrow strip of land connecting two larger land masses. An isthmus is surrounded by water on two sides.

Jack yard. A *yard* which spans above the gaff, giving the topsail a greater span.

Jackstaff. Flag staff at the *bowsprit*, or on the bow of the boat.

Jackstay. Lines along the ship's *yard* to which the sail is fastened. This line moves up and down the mast, thereby raising or lowering the sail.

Jacob's ladder. A collapsible ladder usually used to board a boat. It is made of rope and wood.

Jamming cleat. Device used to secure jib sheet or main sheet.

Jam cleat. This fitting is equipped with two small spring-loaded blocks of wood which together form a V-shaped cleat. A line can be pulled through the V of the cleat, but cannot pass back through without unjamming the line, removing the line from the jaws of the cleat.

Jetty. A protective wall built at the mouth of a river or an open harbour or beach.

Jib. A headsail, or forward sail, that is triangular in shape.

Jibe. See *gibe*.

Jigger. A small tackle or sail.

Jury rig. A rig set up for immediate use during a sea emergency.

Keckling. Material, usually old rope, that is wrapped around lines to prevent chaffing.

Kedge. (1) A light anchor. (2) To propel a boat by means of dragging an anchor.

Keel. The main *timber* or foundation of a vessel; also the name given to the protruding timber which extends lengthwise along the bottom of a vessel.

Keel haul. To drag a person beneath the keel of a boat. No longer practised, this was once punishment used during times of war.

Keelson. A *timber* which is bolted to the keel of the boat for additional support. A "cross keelson" is a timber which is placed across the keelson to give support to the keel where heavy machinery might be placed.

Ketch. A two-masted sailboat. The taller mast is forward and the smaller aftermast is forward of the tiller or wheel.

Key (*or* cay). A low island or reef.

Kicking strap. A line, usually of metal, running from the bottom of the mast, used to hold the boom down.

Knee. A piece of wood which connects the *frames* to the *beams*.

Knot. A unit of speed equalling one nautical mile per hour. A nautical mile is an inexact measurement. It is based on the length of a minute arc (one sixtieth of a degree) of the great circle of the earth. It is not exact because the earth is not a perfect sphere. The international nautical mile, to which the U.S. has subscribed since 1959, equals 6076.115 feet or 1852 metres. The British nautical mile equals 6080 feet or 1853.2 metres.

Labour. When a boat pitches and rolls in a particularly heavy sea, she is said to labour.

Lacing. A line used to secure the sail to the mast or boom, or to secure two sections of a sail, or sunshade, together.

Ladder. A stairway.

Lagoon. A shallow body of water, as a pond or lake, which usually has a shallow, restricted outlet to the sea.

Lake. Any standing body of inland water, generally of considerable size.

Land ho! A familiar exclamation which acknowledges the presence of land.

Land-fall. A vessel's movement towards, and subsequent contact with the shore. A "good land-fall" is to reach the destination as planned.

Landlocked. Surrounded by land.

Landlubber. A person who is uncomfortable on and unfamiliar with a boat; therefore, a person who remains only on land.

Lanyard. A short line or cord used for securing small articles, such as a pail or knife.

Larboard. The port-side of a boat (obsolete term). The opposite of starboard.

Lash. To tie down lines, or tie down objects in a boat; to secure with line.

Lateral mark. A navigation buoy marking a channel.

Latitude. The distance, measured in degrees, which is north or south of the Equator.

Launch. (1) To place a vessel in water. (2) A large, open, power boat.

Lay. To go to an assigned position or station aboard a boat.

Lazarette. Storage space that is located in the stern of a boat.

Lazy. Spare.

Lead line. A lightweight line which is marked off in intervals, and has lead attached to the end. When dropped overboard, it measures the depth of water.

Leading light/marks. Lights or marks which when lined up indicate the best approach to a port.

League. A unit of measurement which equals 3 nautical miles.

Leaning out. To lean over that side of a vessel which is out of the water when heeling. This action counteracts exaggerated heeling by redistributing the weight in the boat. Sometimes known as hiking.

Lee. The side of the boat which is opposite from that side on which the winds blow. The side sheltered from the wind.

Lee helm. A boat carries lee helm if she tends to drift off the wind.

Leeboard. A board which is placed on the side of a boat so as to prevent the boat from drifting leeward.

Leech. The aft edge of a sail.

Leech line. A line which is used to hoist the leech of the sail.

Lee shore. Shore onto which the wind is blowing.

Leeward. Away from the wind.

Leeway. The leeward drift of a boat caused by winds and/or tides.

Lie to. Said of a boat which is underway, yet makes no progress in any direction.

Life-lines. Safety lines permanently attached to, or stowed on any part of a vessel that passengers or crew may hold onto. They are usually located along the gunwale.

Lift. (1) A line suspended from the masthead. It supports the boom and raises its end. (2) A shift of wind allowing a boat to point higher.

Limber board. A plank which covers the limbers in order to keep them free of dirt so that they will not become clogged. Should clogging occur, overflow usually ensues.

Limber chain. A chain kept in the limbers to keep them clean and clear; also called a limber clearer.

Limber holes. Holes which are drilled fore and aft. They allow the bilge water to flow.

Limber strake. The width of planks at the keelson in the hull of a boat.

Line. Any rope which is used aboard a vessel.

List. To lean to one side, or to heel.

LOA. A standard abbreviation for length overall. The longest measurement from bow to stern, as opposed to length at the waterline.

Locker. Storage area aboard a vessel.

Log. An instrument that records the speed of a boat.

Logbook. A journal or book which serves as a complete record of all the boat's activities, including winds encountered, speed, ports docked in, and the like.

Longitude. The degree of distance east or west of the meridian of Greenwich, England.

Lookout. A member of the crew, usually stationed at the bow or aloft, who reports conditions.

Loom. (1) The section of an oar located between the handle and the blade. (2) The distortion of size and distance of a light as seen through a fog or mist.

Loose footed sail. A sail which is not attached to the boom at the foot of the mast.

Lubber line. A compass mark which indicates fore and aft.

Luff. A sail luffs when it shakes violently, like a sheet in the wind. This happens when a boat is in *irons*; when a boat points too close to the wind; or when a sail is let out too far. The forward edge of a sail is also called a luff.

Luff up. To head into the wind.

Luff tackle. A large tackle constructed of both a single and double block that moves freely.

Lugger. A small boat rigged with lugsails.

Lugsail. A sail with four corners and no boom. It is rigged by hanging it from the mast, and attaching it to an upper yard.

Lurch. The sudden pitching and rolling of a boat.

LWL. A standard abbreviation for length waterline. The length of a vessel as measured at the waterline.

Mackinaw boat. A sailboat with a flat bottom and a pointed bow. It can be a *double-ender*.

Magnetic compass. A pivoted navigational aid which indicates geographical directions by a magnet that interacts with the earth's natural magnetic field.

Main beam. The beam located in front of the main hatch.

Main deck. The foremost deck aboard a boat. The term is usually used in reference to larger boats.

Main yard. The spar upon which the mainsail rests.

Main/mainsail. The principal sail aboard a boat.

Mainmast. The principal mast on a boat.

Mainsheet. A line which controls and is hitched to the mainsail.

Mainstay. A cable which supports the mast.

Make. To make is also to reach port. When a tide is making it is getting higher. To make sails is to set them; to make fast is to secure a line.

Man. To man a ship is to ready it for use, by employing crew members.

Manrope. Lines used to climb up the sides of a boat; in function, similar to that of a handrail.

Marina. A facility that offers boaters such services as dock space, moorings, water, and fuel.

Marks. An indexing mark on a leadline which indicates the depth of the water when the line is submerged.

Marline. A small line made of two yarns which have been twisted together; it is used to marl so as to prevent chafing of lines and ropes.

Marlinespike. An iron device which separates the line during splicing.

Marry. To splice two lines together.

Martingale. A short spar spreading downward from the bowsprit aboard a sailboat. Also called a dolphin striker.

Mast. A long vertical spar on a boat to which sails and rigging are attached.

Master. The skipper or captain in charge of a vessel.

Masthead. The top of the mast.

Masthouse. A building in which masts are made, worked on, and repaired.

Mat. A padding or woven rope which prevents continued chafing of rigging.

Mate. A member of the crew ranking directly below the captain; second in command.

Mayday. A general, internationally known term that is a distress signal conveyed by radio. Derived from "M'aidez," the French expression for "Help me."

Meridian. North-South line through any point.

Mercator projection. A well known and frequently used chart on which the earth is shown on a rectangular surface.

Messenger. A line used to haul heavy ropes or lines.

Midsea. A wide, open space in the sea where other ships and land are absent.

Midships. (1) The widest part of a vessel; also called *amidships.* (2) The planks at the broadest point of a boat.

Mile. A mile on a boat is longer than a mile on land. A nautical mile equals 6076.115 feet or 1852 metres. See _knot_.

Mizzen. The stern sail on a ketch or yawl.

Mizzenmast. A mast which supports the mizzen. It is located in the stern of a boat.

Monkey block. A block that is strapped with a _swivel_.

Moor. To secure a boat to a mooring.

Mooring. An anchoring device that permanently holds a boat in a particular spot in the water. It is used instead of a dock.

Mooring buoy. A small buoy at the end of a mooring line. It can be picked up by a boat hook when mooring. Also known as a pick-up buoy.

Mooring block. A large, iron piece which anchors or moors a boat in a particular place in the water, and most often in a harbour.

Mop. A broom made of old rags or yarn that is used to swab the decks of a boat.

Motorsailer. A boat which is designed to move well under power, but is also rigged for sailing. It is usually a large vessel.

Mouse. A knot used on an eye or a hook in order to prevent slipping.

Mouth. The exit or point of discharge of a stream into another stream, lake, or sea.

Mushroom anchor. A cupped anchor with no flukes. It is designed to sink into a mud bottom, and is most often for a permanent mooring.

Nautical. Referring to anything which pertains to seafaring or the sea.

Nautical almanac. An almanac with information pertaining to sea navigation.

Nautical mile. 6076.115 feet or 1852 metres. See *knot.*

Navigation. The proficient guiding of a vessel safely to its predetermined destination; the calculation of a ship's course.

Neap tide. That tide occurring approximately once a month in which there is the least amount of change from high to low in comparison to the other tides of that month.

Neaped. Refers to a ship which goes aground because of *neap tides*; when this condition occurs, it is necessary to wait for the high tide.

Near. Towards the wind. In a boat's world there are two movements which are important, that of the boat itself and that of the wind. A boat is near when its movement is 'near' to opposite the movement of the wind.

Netting. Small lines woven into nets which are used for stowing gear such as hammocks and sails.

Nose. The stem of a vessel.

Nut. Projections on either side of an anchor.

Oakum. Caulking fibres made of old unravelled lines.

Oar. A long, thin wooden pole with a flatbladed end; it is used to row small boats.

Oarlock. The cup-like device which holds the oar in place while it is in use. An oarlock is located on the gunwale, close to the middle of the boat.

Occutting. A flashing navigational light, where the periods when the light is on are longer than the periods when the light is off.

Off. Away from the shore; as in the expression, to sail a mile off shore.

Off the wind. Not close hauled.

Offing. At a distance from the shore, yet in sight; for example, a point far out at sea, yet still visible from the shore.

Offshore. Away from the land.

Offshore wind. A wind which blows from the land towards the sea.

Outboard. An engine that is mounted temporarily on the stern of a boat, usually a small one.

Outhaul. A rope used to haul out the corner of a sail.

Outlet. The opening by or through which any body of water discharges its contents.

Outrigger. A spar which extends outward from the boat, and functions in a variety of ways.

Overboard. In the water.

Overhaul. (1) To separate tackle blocks by pulling them. (2) to check the rigging. (3) The expression once meant to examine the ship carefully and thoroughly for contraband.

Painter. A line which is used to secure or tow a smaller boat like a dinghy.

Palm. (1) A thimble of leather or metal which is used for work on sails or lines. (2) Also a term used for the anchor's *fluke*.

Parbuckle. To lower or hoist by means of two single lines.

Parcel. Taping used around the ends of a rope. It is made of canvas which has been tarred.

Parrel. An iron band which secures the *yard* to the mast, and allows the yard to run smoothly up and down the mast.

Part. The breaking of a rope, or chain, or parts of a cable.

Partner. A timber which supports the mast and the section of the deck upon which the mast rests. This section requires additional support.

Pawl. An iron device which permits rotation in only one direction. It functions, for example, to steady the *capstan.*

Pay. (1) When the bow of a vessel *falls off* from the wind, it is said to be paying off. (2) Also, to fill a seam with tar-like pitch or a similar compound.

Pay out. To ease out a rope.

Peak. The outer and upper corner of a sail common to a gaff rigged boat.

Peninsula. A body of land jutting into, and nearly surrounded on all sides by water; it is frequently (but not necessarily) connected to a larger body of land by a neck or isthmus.

Pennant. (1) *Tackle* which is used to receive goods on board; also known as a pendant. (2) Also, a small, slender flag.

Pick-up buoy. See *mooring buoy.*

Pier. A structure which extends into the water from shore, and functions like a dock. It is supported by pilings, and is usually longer than a wharf.

Piling. A timber or a log which stands vertically in the water. It is stuck into the bottom and protrudes out of the water. It supports docks and piers, and serves other similar purposes.

Pillow. A support which is located at the bowsprit's inner edge.

Pin/pin rail. An iron or wood piece which is used for *belaying* lines. It is fitted with pins so that lines can be secured.

Pinch. To sail into the wind to the extent that the sails are luffing.

Pindjajap. A boat of Sumatra origin that is square-rigged, and generally carries two sails. It is used as an import boat to carry spices; sometimes it is rigged as a pleasure boat used in European areas.

Pinnace. A small boat, often sailed in conjunction with a large sailboat.

Pintle. A metal bolt which functions as a support for the rudder. It is a swinging support, and is attached to the rudder.

Pitch. (1) A sticky, tar-like substance used to fill boat seams and intersecting points on a boat. (2) Also, to rock back and forth (from bow to stern) with each end going down into the water alternately.

Pivoting point. The point at which a vessel turns. The point varies from boat to boat.

Planks. Sturdy boards which are used in the construction of the boat. They cover the hull deck, and the sides of a vessel.

Plot. To calculate a course on a chart.

Point. (1) Any of the thirty-two marks which indicate all directions on the compass card of a compass. (2) To point a rope is to work a rope's end so that it flows smoothly through a block without unravelling. (3) To sail close or near the wind.

Point up. To steer a boat closer to the wind.

Pond. A small, fresh-water lake.

Pool. (1) A water hole or small pond; (2) A small body of standing water. (3) A small and rather deep body of (usually) fresh water, as in a stream.

Poop. (1) A deck found on board sailboats. It is raised and is often located in the stern of the boat. (2) When waves break over the stern of the boat.

Poppets. A timber used to support a vessel during launching.

Port. (1) Towards the bow, the left side, and all parts of a vessel which are to the left of the centreline are on the port side. (2) Also a place to dock or anchor a boat safely.

Porthole. A window or opening which permits air to flow through the boat. It is located on the side of the boat.

Port tack. A sailboat's world is divided in half by the wind. Each half is called a tack. If a boat's sails are on the port or left side of the boat, the boat is on port tack.

Prayer book. A scrubbing stone used on board a boat.

Preventer. Extra lines which secure the vessel and its various parts during heavy gales and storms.

Pricker. A marlinespike used in the making of rigging and sails.

Privileged vessel. The vessel with the right of way. The other vessel is the burdened vessel.

Propeller. A bladed device secured to the shaft of a vessel. It propels the boat.

Pulpit rail. Safety tubing extending around the bow rail.

Pushpit rail. Safety tubing extending around the stern rail.

Purchase. Another term for tackle.

Quarter. The section of a vessel, either on port or starboard, which is between *midships* and *astern*.

Quarter-block. A block through which sheets and lines travel; it is attached to the yard.

Quarter-deck. Part of the upper deck in the stern of the boat; originally located between the mainmast and the poopdeck.

Quarters. The areas for living and sleeping aboard.

Quay. A wharf which is used primarily for the handling of cargo; it is usually made of cement, to accommodate heavy cargo.

Race. A strong channel or current of water.

Rack. To fasten two lines together by twisting them around each other.

Rack-block. A series of blocks, all made from one section of wood, through which lines run.

Radar. An electronic detection device that determines bearing and size of objects by their reflection of radio signals.

Radio beacon. See *beacon*.

Rail. The top of the bulwarks located above the deck.

Range. The difference in heights between low and high tide.

Rake. The slanting of a mast of a vessel both fore and aft.

Rat lines. Lines which are lashed horizontally between the shrouds of a vessel so as to form a ladder for climbing aloft; (often used for a lookout).

Reach. (1) When a boat is sailing with the wind abeam it is said to be sailing on a beam reach. (2) A broad reach is with the wind *abaft*. (3) A close reach is one with the wind forward of the beam, yet not close-hauled.

Ready about. To stand by to come about or change tack; a warning that the boom is going to swing from one side to the other, as the boat comes about.

Ready to gibe. The skipper's warning that he is going to gibe.

Reckoning. The calculation of a ship's position with use of navigational tools.

Reef. To shorten or lessen a sail area.

Reef band. A piece of canvas which is sewn across the sail to facilitate *reefing*.

Reef knot. A commonly used square knot.

Reef tackle. A tackle which is used to hoist the leech up the yard. This is an aide in reefing a sail.

Reeve. To pass a line, or the end of a line, through a block, or to secure a line with the aid of a block.

Regatta. Boat races usually sponsored by a yacht club.

Render. To make sure that a line flows smoothly through a block without tangling.

Ribbands. Timbers used to temporarily hold together the ribs of a boat during the construction of a boat. They are placed around the existing framework to hold it in position.

Ribs. The timbers which form the vessel's frame.

Ride. To be anchored, as in the expression, "the boat was riding near the shore."

Riders. Additional timbers placed on the inside of the ship's frame that add extra strength to the frame.

Riding light. Anchor light.

Rig. A descriptive term which differentiates between types of sailboats, and the arrangement of their masts and sails. It also means to set up, as to rig a boat.

Rigging. Refers to all cables, lines, and ropes which are used on board a vessel. It can also refer to the shrouds. (1) Standing rigging remains permanent or fixed. (2) Running rigging is made fast at one end and can move at the other to control sails, booms, and other moveable parts of a vessel.

Right. (1) To set the helm amidships. (2) Also, to turn a capsized boat upright.

Ring. The upper part of an anchor to which the cable is fastened.

Ring bolt. A bolt made of iron with a ring at its head.

Ring tail (ring sail). A small sail, which is light and shaped like a jib. It is used to extend sails during light winds.

Rip. A body of water which becomes rough because of conflicting currents or an irregular bottom.

Risings. Planks which are placed fore and aft in a small open boat. They accommodate pads or pillows which function as seats.

River. A natural stream of running water, larger than a creek or a brook.

Roach. The section of the sail which is curved. It is located at the foot of the sail, and prevents the sail from tangling with lines and stays.

Roadstead. A place of anchorage in an open space, usually at some distance from the shore.

Rode. Another term for the anchor line is the anchor-rode.

Roll. The side to side swaying of a vessel; or, to sway side to side.

Roller reef. Reducing the sail area by rolling the bottom of the sail around the boom.

Rope. A cord usually more than one inch in thickness. Aboard a sailboat, a rope is known as a line.

Row. To propel a boat by using oars.

Row-locks. Recesses in which the oars rest while they are in use.

Royal. A small sail used only during light winds.

Rubbing strake. A piece of wood to take the wear when a boat is moored to a jetty.

Rudder. The instrument which is attached to the stern of the boat. It controls the direction of a boat.

Rules of the road. International rules and regulations which make boating and navigation safe; they are universally understood. They concern such subjects as the side on which one enters a channel, the side on which a buoy is placed, and the right of way. In references to the latter, the rules are: sailboat over canoe, canoe over rowboat, rowboat over inboard, and inboard over outboard.

Run. (1) A boat sailing directly with wind is on a "dead run"; if it sails close to a dead run, it is on a run. (2) A small, swift brook or creek. (3) The aft section of the hull, where it begins to curve upward.

Runabout. A small, open power boat.

Rungheads. The upper section of the floor of a boat.

Running lights. Lights which are fastened onto a boat for navigational purposes, safety, and use during the hours of darkness.

Sag. To drift leeward.

Sailboat. A boat which is propelled by wind which fills the sails.

Sailcloth. The material of which sails are made.

Sails. Sheets made of Dacron or canvas or other material; they are placed on a vessel to catch the wind, thus moving the vessel. Square sails are shaped like a square and are hung from their middle onto a *yard*. Fore and aft sails are set onto a boom and run with their feet lined up with the boat's keel. To set the sail is to hoist it in preparation for sailing. To shorten the sail is to tighten it in order to lessen the degree to which the sail works. To be under sail is, simply, to sail.

Sampan. A small boat used primarily in the Orient. It is propelled by rowing from the stern; often, a sail of some sort is used for additional power.

Samson post. A single timber used for securing lines on the bow of a small boat.

Saveall. A small sail which is rigged beneath a larger sail in order to catch all the wind that would otherwise pass beneath the larger sail. Sometimes called a catch-all.

Scantlings. The dimensions of a vessel's timbers.

Schooner. A boat whose rigging includes two or more masts.

Scope. The length of anchor line which has been played out.

Score. A groove or rut that runs in a block.

Scraper. A device which is shaped like a triangle; it is used for cleaning and scraping decks, masts, etc.

Screw. Another word for the propeller of a boat.

Scull. A short oar. To scull is to use the oar at the stern of a boat, moving it in sudden or swift, short sidestrokes.

Scuppers. Holes at the side of the boat, or at deck level, which allow water to drain off at the deck. Sometimes these are called scupperholes.

Scuttle. (1) A small hatch. (2) To scuttle a boat is to purposely sink it by cutting holes in her.

Sea. (1) A large body of salt water, second in rank to an ocean. It is more or less landlocked and generally part of, or connected with, an ocean, or a larger sea. (2) The term may also refer to the condition, size, or strength of the waves: for example, a choppy sea; or a long sea (one characterised by many swells).

Sea anchor. An anchor which is dragged from the stern of a boat in order to hold the boat to the wind.

Seachannel. A long, narrow, shallow U-shaped or V-shaped depression of the sea floor, usually occurring on a gently sloping plain or fan.

Seacock. A safety valve on, near, or below water line fittings. Seacocks are used to cut off the entry of water in case of leakage and when repairs on equipment must be made.

Seams. The section between the intersection of planks or timbers, on the side or deck of a boat.

Seaward. Away from the shore or towards the sea.

Seaway. Part of the sea which is rough.

Secure. To make fast.

Seize. To make fast lines by means of wrapping small pieces of cord or yarn around them.

Sennit (sinnet). A braid which is made by plaiting or weaving rope together in a pattern.

Serve. To fasten lines together by wrapping; the term is used interchangeably with seize.

Set. (1) To tighten rigging. (2) The set of a current is the direction in which it flows. (3) To move in a particular direction, as with the flow of the tide or the current.

Shackles. A U-shaped device made of metal. It has two eyes at its end through which a pin, the shackle pins, closes it off. It links together two pieces of chain or cable.

Shakedown. A trial cruise to determine a boat's fitness.

Shank. The part of the anchor that is between the arms and the stock. This is the main section of the anchor.

Shank painter. A strong cable which holds the arms and the stock of the anchor to the side of the boat.

She. The nautical reference to a boat.

Sheathing. A covering on the bottom of a boat. It protects the areas where barnacles tend to attach themselves.

Sheave. The wheel inside of a block through which the line runs.

Sheer. (1) The lengthwise sweep of the boat, following the line of the deck. (2) A quick change in course.

Sheer strake. The uppermost plank or *strake* of the vessel's hull. Also known as the paint strake.

Sheet. Lines which control the sails and the motion of the boom.

Sheet anchor. An anchor on larger boats which is carried amidships. It is the largest aboard a boat, and is used in emergencies.

Sheet bend. A knot which fastens a line to an eye.

Ship. (1) A large vessel with three or four masts. (2) To take on board, e.g. to ship water.

Shipshape. The neat and orderly appearance of a vessel.

Shivering. Shaking or luffing of a sail because the wind cuts its edge.

Shoal. An off-shore hazard to navigation with a maximum depth of ten fathoms. It is composed of unconsolidated material.

Shock cord. A piece of elastic covered with cotton used to secure various articles aboard a boat. It often secures a furled sail to the boom.

Shore. The narrow zone of land fronting any body of water.

Shoreline. The line of contact between the land and a body of water.

Shorten. To reduce the sail area by pulling in the sheets or by reefing.

Shove off. To depart, as in leaving a dock and pushing off the pilings. This is a common term used by boating people.

Shrouds. Wires or lines which support the mast; they are placed at the mast and run down onto both sides of the boat.

Side lights. Running lights on the port and starboard sides of the boat; the port light is red, and the starboard light is green.

Sill. A ridge or rise separating partially closed basins from one another, or from the adjacent sea floor.

Sister block. A piece of wood with two sheaves and a core for seizing.

Sister ship. Another ship of same class, size, or line.

Skeg. (1) Planks or timbers which extend or deepen the aft section of the keel. (2) A wood or metal projection which extends the propeller or rudder of a boat.

Skysail. A very light sail which is rigged above the royal sail on board a square-rigged mast.

Slablines. A line which takes up slack that runs through a block.

Slack. The part of a line which hangs loosely. To take in or pull in the slack is to tighten the *sheet*.

Slack water. A slow moving current. To navigate by slack water is to navigate in small streams.

Sling. (1) A line in which materials can be hoisted and lowered. (2) A line which secures the *yard's* centre to the mast of the boat.

Slip. (1) An area between two pilings on a pier or a dock; boats are docked in this space instead of a mooring. (2) A slanted platform from which boats are placed into or hoisted out of the water. (3) To let go of a line, as in the expression "to slip an anchor."

Slip rope. A line which is bent to the anchor rode at the hawse hole; it is used in preparation for slipping.

Sloop. A one-masted boat usually rigged with a jib and a main. It is differentiated from a *cutter* on the basis of its mast, which is closer to the bow, and a single mainsail.

Sloop of war. A term used to refer to a sailboat (although not necessarily sloop-rigged) containing mountings for anywhere up to 32 guns. In more modern use, it refers to any warship rigged with guns on one side.

Smack. A small sailboat usually with sloop rigging; it functions as a coastline fishing boat also known as smack boat.

Small craft warning. An indication that weather conditions make it dangerous to sail a small boat. A red pennant indicates such conditions.

Snake. To spirally twist a smaller line round another larger rope by interspersing the smaller with the strands of the rope.

Snap shackle. A shackle with a spring catch.

Snap block. A single block with an opening on one side which receives the bight of the rope. The opening is below the sheave.

Snub. To suddenly stop a rope.

Sny. The upward bend of the plank in the frame of the boat that accounts for the upward bend in the boat's lines.

Sole. An extra piece located at the lower end of the rudder to make it level with the keel.

Sound. (1) To determine the water's depth with an electronic device. A sounding is the actual depth found. (2) Off soundings refers to water which is deep enough to make it impossible to reach the bottom with lead and line. (3) A protected body of water between an island and the coast. The usually calm sea and steady wind make for good sailing.

Span. A rope or line used to secure various parts to the boat, such as the boom.

Spanker. The after sail of the schooner which has more than three masts.

Spars. Any poles used in support such as masts, booms, yards, sprits, and gaffs. Anything which is used in the support of the sails.

Speak. To communicate with a vessel which is at sea.

Speaking trumpet. A flare-mouthed tube which is often used on board a boat to communicate with other members of the crew or other boats.

Spencer. A fore and aft sail rigged without a boom. A spencer-mast is the mast from which the spencer is hoisted and set just aft of the fore and main masts.

Spill. To empty a sail of its wind.

Spilling line. A line used in rough weather to spill a sail. It may also be used to furl a sail.

Spindrift. The spray blown from the tops of the waves when the sea is exceptionally rough. The sea's surface becomes covered with this spray. Also called spoondrift.

Spinnaker. A light, triangular sail, used primarily in racing, when running before the wind. It is rigged on a boom extending over the side of the boat and opposite the main boom. It is an exceptionally large sail and spreads over the boat.

Splice. To join two ropes into a single line by weaving strands from each line together.

Spray. The water which is blown from the tops of the waves.

Spreaders. Bars of metal or iron used to spread stays, shrouds, and other similar pieces. Also used as a mast support.

Spring. (1) To crack or strain a mast. (2) To spring a leak is to create a leak aboard the boat. (3) To spring a luff is to bring the sail or the boat closer to the wind.

Spring line. A line attached at one end to the side of the boat. The other side is attached to a dock to inhibit the boat's movement. It also prevents the bow and the stern from touching the dock. In addition, it is used to pull the boat closer to the dock for loading and unloading.

Spring stay. (1) A support for a principal stay. (2) A horizontal stay on a schooner.

Spring tides. After the new and the full moon, the highest tide of the month.

Sprit. A boom or spar used to extend the fore and aft sail; extends diagonally from the mast.

Spritsail. A sail which is extended or rigged from a sprit.

Spritsail yard. A yard upon which the spritsail is rigged; a yard which spans across the bowsprit to spread the guys of the jib.

Spunyarn. A line which is made by twisting or weaving two or three rope yarns together.

Spur. A curved timber which is a half beam used to support the deck in the area that cannot accommodate an entire beam.

Spurling line. The line which communicates between the helm and the telltale.

Squall. A violent blast of wind, or a sudden storm. Often, a squall occurs without warning during a seemingly clear sky. Its primary features are high winds and heavy rains.

Square. Equipment which forms right angles with the keel and the mast, such as the yards.

Square sail. A sail which is square in shape, spans to a yard, and is hung from the middle.

Square-rigged. A boat that carries most of its sails athwart-ships without the use of booms, gaffs, and stays. Instead it is rigged by extending the sails from their middle.

Squat. Position of the boat when its bow is raised. This condition is a result of movement at a high speed which forces the stern down into the water.

Stability. A vessel's stiffness.

Staff. A pole on which a flag or light is hoisted.

Stanchions. Upright posts of metal or wood used to support a boat's beams. They also hold the lifelines.

Stand. The period of time at which the tide remains at a consistent level, being neither high nor low.

Stand by. (1) To be prepared to follow orders. (2) A command given when the skipper is ready to come about. (3) Informs crew members that tack is about to be changed.

Standing rigging. That rigging which holds the masts and spars of a boat.

Starboard. When facing the bow of the boat, the area to the right of the centreline is the starboard side of the boat.

Starboard tack. Opposite of *port tack*. When the sails of a boat are set on the right or starboard side of the boat, it is on a starboard tack.

Stay. To change a boat's tack so that the wind catches the other side of the boat.

Stays. Wires or ropes which support the mast. They lead from the mast's head to some part of the boat. Stays which go forward are called fore-and-aft stays. Stays which lead to the boat's side are called back-stays.

Staysail. A triangular sail which is from a stay.

Steady. To keep the helm in its present position.

Steerage. The section of the boat just forward of the cabin.

Steerageway. The minimum or slowest speed at which a boat may operate, with the helm or rudder still responding, and the entire boat being controlled.

Stem. The timber most forward in the boat's hull that is also the most forward beam of the keel which reaches up to the bow. The expression "from stem to stern", means from one end of a boat to the other.

Step. A block of wood which secures the heel of the mast. It is placed in the keel on the boats where the mast reaches the *hull*.

Step the mast. To raise the mast after it has been taken down for winter, storage, or repairs.

Stern. The section of a boat opposite the bow, or the after end of a vessel.

Stern fast. A line used in docking, leading off the stern of the boat.

Stern foremost. An awkward position in which the stern comes forward.

Stern frame. The section of the hull which forms the skeleton of the stern of the boat.

Stern sheets. An open area in the stern of the boat that accommodates passengers.

Sternmost. Closest to the stern.

Sternpost. The main piece of timber used in the frame of the stern. The rudder is secured to this timber.

Sternward. Towards the stern.

Sternway. The backward movement of a boat.

Stevedore. The member of the crew who is in charge of the loading and unloading of cargo.

Stiff. The ability of a boat to carry a large amount of sail without leaning greatly to one side.

Stinkpot. A term used by many pleasure boat sailors which refers to power boats and their need to rely on fuel which pollutes the waters. A stinkpotter is a person who owns or uses a stinkpot.

Stirrups. A rope with eyes that is secured to a yard.

Stools. A groove at the side of the boat in which the dead eyes of the back stays lie.

Stopper. A short piece of rope that is knotted at one end, and sometimes has a hook at the other end. It is used for securing lines.

Stopper bolt. A large bolt which is placed in the deck, and to which the stopper is secured.

Stops. (1) Projections on the lower mast outside of the cheeks. (2) To stop is to make fast.

Stores. Refers to anything on board a boat that will be used for a specific purpose; all foods, paint, varnishes, etc.

Storm jib. A small sail at the bow used during heavy seas.

Stove. A vessel is said to be stove when the side of her has been smashed from the outside.

Stow. To store away in an organised or compact fashion, as in the expression, "to stow away gear."

Strait. A relatively narrow body of water connecting two larger bodies.

Strake. Planks which run fore and aft in a boat rather than across it.

Strand. (1) A number of yarns which are twisted together; three, four, or nine twisted yarns is a rope. (2) A vessel is stranded when it is aground or near shore; to purposely strand a boat near shore is to beach a boat. (3) The shore or beach of the ocean or a large lake.

Strap. A piece of iron looped and placed around a block. This holds the block together so that it can be hung.

Stream. Any body, great or small, of flowing water or other fluid.

Stream anchor. An anchor which is usually lighter than a mooring anchor. It is used for warping.

Stream channel. The bed where a natural stream of water runs; the trench or depression washed in the surface of the earth by running water; a wash.

Stretchers. (1) A narrow plank that is placed on the bottom of a boat. It serves as a foot rest for those who row the boat. (2) A cross-piece timber which keeps the boat's sides apart.

Strike. To lower the sails.

Stringers. Long, horizontal planks that are fastened to interior ribs of the boat. They support the beam.

Strip. To unrig or dismantle a boat.

Strut. An arm that holds the propeller shaft in line.

Studdingsails. Sails that are used only during light winds. They are additional sails that are rigged on the outside of the square sails and fastened to an extended boom whose function is to hold the rigging of the studdingsails.

Supporter. Timbers under the *cathead*. Also called the bibb.

Surf. Refers to the sea as it breaks at the shoreline.

Swab. A mop made from old ropes. It is used to scrub and clean decks.

Swage. A metal terminal pressed onto a wire rope.

Swamp. To take water over the side of the boat, in order to sink it, or to sink it just below the surface of the water.

Sway. To raise or hoist.

Sweep. A long oar that is used on small boats.

Swells. Long, rounded waves caused by strong winds which affect a specific area of the sea. They differ from breaking waves in that a swell is rounded and smooth. They often signal the approach of a major storm.

Swifter. (1) To tighten the *shrouds*. (2) A shroud which runs from the lower mast's head to the side of the ship.

Swig. (1) A tackle whose lines are not parallel. (2) To tighten for hauling.

Swivel. A long, metal link that is used in cables. It is designed to turn on an axis, thus preventing the cable from becoming twisted.

Sypher. To overlap the planks' edges so that they intersect to form a smooth floor.

Tabling. (1) The joining of two timbers of a boat by grooves and notches. (2) The hem along the edge of the sail through which the bolt-rope is run.

Tackle. Ropes and blocks to give increased pulling power.

Tack. (1) One half of the boat's world as represented by the side of the wind the boat is on. See *port tack, starboard tack.* (2) The zig-zag course a boat travelling upwind takes is called tacking. (3) When a boat is moving closely upwind, it is on a tack or a close-haul. (4) The line that anchors the lower corners of a sail, and the corners of the sail it anchors, are tacks.

Taffrail. The pushpit which goes around the ship's stern.

Tail block. A line which is spliced into a block and made fast to a spar.

Tailing the sheets. Taking up the slack by hand while someone else is manually operating the *winch.*

Tarpaulin. A tar-covered piece of canvas often used to cover open hatches, cockpits etc.

Taut. To tighten a sail or a line, leaving no slack.

Tell-tale(s). (1) A compass that hangs from the ceiling of a cabin. (2) Light pieces of yarn or feathers that are secured to different parts of the rigging to show the direction in which the wind is blowing.

Tend. To watch over an anchored boat to ensure that its lines and cables are not fouled.

Tender. (1) A boat that is not sufficiently stable and, thus, carreens a little too easily. (2) A motorised dinghy used by larger ships or yacht basins and marinas.

Thimble. A ring made of iron or other metal. Its side is concave so that a rope or strap can rest tautly on it.

Throat. The end of a gaff which fits next to the mast.

Thrum. Short strands of yarn, wool, or hemp used to mat pieces of canvas by weaving them, used as a chafing preventer.

Thwarts. Seats that go athwartships in an open boat.

Tidal stream. The movement of part of the ocean caused by the tide.

Tide. The periodic rise and fall of the sea.

Tide race. A section of the water where the tide is running with great speed.

Tide gauge. A device which is used to register the variations in the depth of the tide as it rises and falls.

Tiderip. A swirling motion of the water caused by currents running in opposite directions.

Tideway. The section of a river or channel in which the tide runs most strongly.

Tiller. A long bar of wood or metal that is attached to the top of the rudder. This is used to steer the boat. It appears mostly on smaller sailboats, and is generally located in the stern cockpit of the boat.

Tiller extension. An extension on the handle of the tiller so that the skipper can continue to maintain control while *leaning out*. Sometimes known as hiking stick.

Timber. A term which is used to refer to all large pieces of wood that are used in the process of ship-building. They are bent or curved to form the boat's ribs.

Timber-heads. The ends of timbers which rise above the deck and gunwales. They are used for *belaying* lines.

Toe-strap. Straps connected to the floorboards or centre-board. Crew members can secure their feet under the straps when *leaning out*. Sometimes known as hiking strap.

Toggle. A pin that is placed through the eye of a line to secure it, or to secure it with another line.

Top. The platform that is placed over the lower mast in order to secure and spread the rigging.

Top block. A block that is made of iron and is used in hoisting and lowering the topmast.

Topgallant. A spar or sail that is located above the topmast aboard a boat. It is the third mast above the deck.

Top-hamper. Spars and rigging aboard a sailboat that are kept aloft as they are not needed for immediate use.

Top-light. A single lantern that is used for signalling. It is hung in the high rigging of a boat.

Topmast. The second mast above the deck. It is supported by the lower mast, and supports the topgallant mast.

Topping lift. The line which runs from the mast to the boom's outer end; it hoists and supports the boom.

Top-rope. The line used to hoist and lower the topmasts.

Topsail. On a square-rigger, the sail that is second above the deck.

Topsail yard. The spar on which the topsail is bent.

Topsides. That section of the boat which is above the hull's waterline.

Top-timber. Those timbers that are the highest on the boat's side.

Tow. To drag or carry something, or another boat, behind a boat.

Transducer. An electronic sensor for relaying information to navigational instruments, e.g. depth sounder.

Transoms. Timbers placed across the sternpost forming the flat or slightly curved section of the boat's stern. Sometimes used as a seat for passengers.

Traveller. A metal ring that slides up and down the rigging, or the spar upon which the ring is sliding.

Trend. (1) The wide section at the lower end of the anchor's shank. (2) The angle created while a boat is at anchor, from the line of the keel to the anchor-rode.

Trestle-trees. Two horizontal beams running fore and aft. One lies on either side of a mast and is used to support the crosstrees and top.

Triatic stay. A line secured to the mastheads that is used to fasten hoisting tackle.

Tributary. Any stream which feeds a larger stream or lake.

Trice. To hoist and secure with a small line.

Trim. (1) To trim the sails is to set them in accordance with the wind. (2) The degree to which a boat is balanced, and the manner in which it sits in the water.

Trip. To hoist the anchor so that it is clear of the bottom.

Tripping line. (1) A line that is attached to a spar for lowering it. (2) The line used for tripping the anchor.

Trough. The hollow between one wave and the next. A boat is in trough when it lies in that hollow.

Truck. A circular piece of wood at the top or the head of the mast.

True. An exact geographic direction as opposed to a reading of magnetic north, as in the expression, "true north."

Tumbling home (*or* tumble home). The section of the side of the boat which curves upward and inward towards the centreline.

Turn. To pass a line around a pin and to make it fast.

Turnbuckle. A metal screw which can be tightened and

loosened. It is used for setting up standing rigging.

Tye. A line which is connected to the yard and a tackle; it is used for hoisting.

Typhoon. A violent, hurricane-like storm particular to the Eastern seas.

Unbend. To cast off a line, or to unfasten, as in a sail.

Underway. A boat which is not secured to a mooring, anchor or dock. A boat is underway when moving. When underway without direct control of sails, she is said to be adrift.

Unfurl. To unfold a sail, flag, etc.

Unmoor. To hoist one of two anchors up such that the boat rides on a single anchor.

Up and down. When anchor cable is vertical.

Up anchor. The order to hoist up the anchor.

Vang. A line that is used to steady the *gaff.*

Variation. In reference to a compass reading, the difference between true and magnetic north.

Veer. (1) Action of the wind as it changes direction. (2) To slacken off a line, or to let it run out.

Waif. A flag or pennant used for signalling.

Waist. The amidships part of a boat's deck.

Wake. The path of water which a boat leaves behind her as she moves.

Wales. Planks which run fore and aft along the side of a boat.

Wall-sided. Condition of a boat when her hull runs straight without *tumbling home.*

Ware (*or* wear). To change a boat's direction by carrying the wind over her stern; as opposed to tacking, in which the bow is brought around by the wind. To gibe.

Warp. (1) To move a boat by means of a line that is secured to a fixed object. (2) A line used in warping a boat.

Wash. Waves caused by a boat's progress.

Washboard. A board above the gunwale of a boat whose function is to keep the sea and its spray out of the boat.

Watch. (1) The division of time aboard a boat. There are seven such watches during a 24 hour period, two of which are dog watches. (2) To float, as a buoy does.

Watch tackle. A small tackle with a double block.

Water sail. A *save-all* rigged under the swinging boom.

Waterlogged. To be swamped by water, but still afloat.

Waterway. Long planking on the exterior of the boat.

Way. The movement of a boat through the water. Headway is forward movement. Sternway is backward movement.

Weather. The direction from which the wind is blowing. A weather gauge is the condition of a boat when she is too windward of another boat.

Weather helm. Tendency of a boat to come up into the wind. The opposite of *lee helm.*

Weather roll. The rolling of a boat windward.

Weather side. To the windward.

Weather-bitt. An additional turn of the cable.

Weigh. To haul the anchor up from the bottom.

Well-found. Refers to a boat which is well-equipped.

Wetled surface. The surface of the boat under the water.

Wharf. A wooden structure built at the water's edge used for loading, unloading, and docking.

Wheel. A device that is attached to the rudder and used for steering. It is generally found on larger boats.

Whipping. A method which prevents lines from unravelling by seizing the ends of the line.

Whiskers. The supports for a bowsprit. Also known as whisker stays.

Winch. A *purchase* that has a crank or a wheel at the end which facilitates the pulling in of a sheet or line.

Windlass. Device that is used to *weigh* an anchor. Also called capstan.

Wind-rode. When a boat shifts and rides by the wind's force, as opposed to riding with the currents or tides.

Wind's eye. The exact direction from which the wind is coming.

Windward. The opposite of leeward. Towards the wind.

Wing and wing. A boat is sailing wing and wing when her sails are on both sides of the boat. A difficult position to manoeuvre.

Withe. A metal band that is secured to the end of a boom, and to which another mast or rigging is secured.

Woold. To twist a piece of line around a mast.

Yacht. A boat that is used for pleasure purposes. The opposite would be a workboat, such as a tugboat.

Yard. A spar that is attached at the centre of the mast and runs athwartships.

Yaw. When a boat deviates from a steady course.

Yawl. A small sailboat that has two masts. It is distinguished from a ketch because the mizzen mast is aft the wheel or tiller.

Appendix

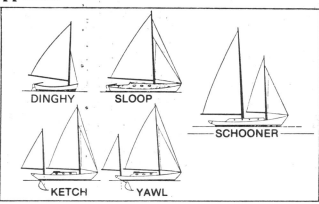

Names of Common Sailing Rigs

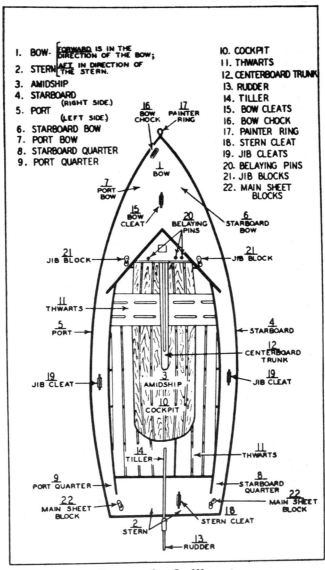

**Parts of a Sailboat
(Deck View)**

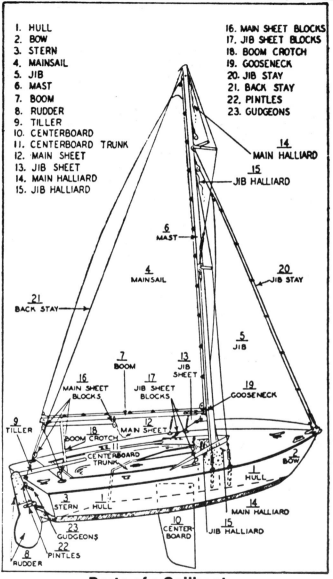

1. HULL
2. BOW
3. STERN
4. MAINSAIL
5. JIB
6. MAST
7. BOOM
8. RUDDER
9. TILLER
10. CENTERBOARD
11. CENTERBOARD TRUNK
12. MAIN SHEET
13. JIB SHEET
14. MAIN HALLIARD
15. JIB HALLIARD
16. MAIN SHEET BLOCKS
17. JIB SHEET BLOCKS
18. BOOM CROTCH
19. GOOSENECK
20. JIB STAY
21. BACK STAY
22. PINTLES
23. GUDGEONS

14 MAIN HALLIARD
15 JIB HALLIARD
6 MAST
4 MAINSAIL
20 JIB STAY
21 BACK STAY
5 JIB
7 BOOM
13 JIB SHEET
16 MAIN SHEET BLOCKS
17 JIB SHEET BLOCKS
19 GOOSENECK
9 TILLER
18 BOOM CROTCH
12 MAIN SHEET
11 CENTERBOARD TRUNK
2 BOW
1 HULL
3 STERN
1 HULL
14 MAIN HALLIARD
10 CENTERBOARD
15 JIB HALLIARD
23 GUDGEONS
22 PINTLES
8 RUDDER

**Parts of a Sailboat
(Side View)**

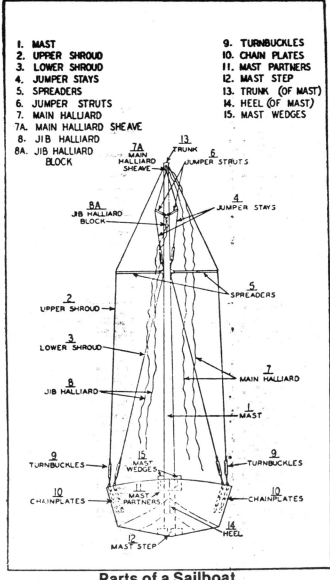

1. MAST
2. UPPER SHROUD
3. LOWER SHROUD
4. JUMPER STAYS
5. SPREADERS
6. JUMPER STRUTS
7. MAIN HALLIARD
7A. MAIN HALLIARD SHEAVE
8. JIB HALLIARD
8A. JIB HALLIARD BLOCK

9. TURNBUCKLES
10. CHAIN PLATES
11. MAST PARTNERS
12. MAST STEP
13. TRUNK (OF MAST)
14. HEEL (OF MAST)
15. MAST WEDGES

**Parts of a Sailboat
(Rigging)**

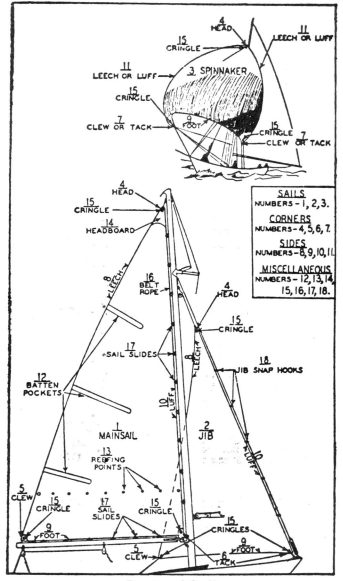

Parts of Sails

Star

The Language OF PHOTOGRAPHY

If you don't know your hot-shoe from your hardener, your shutter release from your SLR, or your safelight from your self-timer – THE LANGUAGE OF PHOTOGRAPHY can save you valuable time and money.

Star

The Language

OF

ASTROLOGY

f you can't tell a conjunction from a configuration, a mean motion from a matutine, or primary directions from points of illumination, THE LANGUAGE OF ASTROLOGY can save you hours of valuable time.

The Language
OF
ACCOUNTANCY

Star

The Language

OF
MARTIAL ARTS

If you don't know aikido from ashi-tori, the cat stance from the crab's claw, or an immovable elbow from inner power — you could save yourself from painful mispronunciation and injury by learning THE LANGUAGE OF MARTIAL ARTS.